THE FLYING LOVER

Kneehigh

THE FLYING LOVERS OF VITEBSK

Written by Daniel Jamieson

OBERON BOOKS
LONDON

WWW.OBERONBOOKS.COM

First published in 2017 by Oberon Books Ltd
521 Caledonian Road, London N7 9RH
Tel: +44 (0) 20 7607 3637 / Fax: +44 (0) 20 7607 3629
e-mail: info@oberonbooks.com
www.oberonbooks.com

PB ISBN: 9781786822871
E ISBN: 9781786822888

Cover by Stem Design; Cover photography by Steve Tanner

Printed and bound by 4edge Limited, UK

Visit www.oberonbooks.com to read more about all our books
and to buy them. You will also find features, author interviews and
news of any author events, and you can sign up for e-newsletters
so that you're always first to hear about our new releases.

The original version of *The Flying Lovers of Vitebsk* was performed as *Birthday* by Theatre Alibi in 1992.

Writer: Daniel Jamieson
Director: Nikki Sved
Designer: Dominie Hooper
Lighting Designer: Paul Tyler
Original Cast: Daniel Jamieson & Emma Rice

The Flying Lovers of Vitebsk is a Kneehigh production in association with Bristol Old Vic. It was first performed at Bristol Old Vic on the 27th May 2016 and first performed in Kneehigh's Asylum on 14th July 2016.

Cast

MARC CHAGALL	Marc Antolin
BELLA CHAGALL	Audrey Brisson
MUSICIAN	Ian Ross
MUSICIAN	James Gow

Creative Team

Writer	Daniel Jamieson
Director	Emma Rice
Composer and Music Director	Ian Ross
Designer	Sophia Clist
Lighting Designer	Malcolm Rippeth
Sound Designer	Simon Baker
Choreographer	Etta Murfitt
Associate Lighting Designer	Victoria Brennan
Assistant Director	Matt Harrison
Executive Producer	Ali Robertson
Producer	Liz King

Technical Team

Company Stage Manager	Steph Curtis
Technical Stage Manager	Aled William Thomas
Assistant Stage Manager	Gemma Gale
Sound Operator	Yamina Mezeli
Costume Supervisor	Ed Parry
Associate Costume Supervisor	Annelies Henry

For Kneehigh

Artistic Director	Mike Shepherd
Executive Producer	Ali Robertson
General Manager & Director of Rambles	Charlotte Bond
Producer	Liz King
Production Manager	David Miller
Company Stage Manager	Steph Curtis
Finance Officer	Fiona Buxton
Development Manager	Bethany Lyne
Marketing & Communications Manager	Teri Laing
Communications Assistant	Dann Carroll
Production Assistant	Millie Jones
Administrator	Taryn Harris
Rambles Lead Artist	Anna Maria Murphy
Press & PR	Clióna Roberts
Photographer	Steve Tanner
Film Maker	Brett Harvey
Illustrator	Daryl Waller

Kneehigh

For thirty-five years Kneehigh have created vigorous, popular and challenging theatre, with a joyful anarchy. We have performed everywhere from village halls to castles, disused quarries to conventional stages all over the world.

From our breath-taking barns in Cornwall we create theatre of humanity on an epic and tiny scale. Led by Mike Shepherd, we work with an ever-changing bunch of talented and like-minded performers, artists, makers and musicians and are passionate about the creative process.

The Asylum, a beautiful nomadic structure, is home to theatre, fun and Kneehigh knees-ups. Alongside major productions and tours we also run the Kneehigh Rambles – fun adventures and magical events with communities in Cornwall and beyond.

www.kneehigh.co.uk

Bristol Old Vic

Bristol Old Vic is the oldest continuously-working theatre in the United Kingdom. Our mission is to create pioneering twenty-first century theatre in partnership with the people of Bristol; inspired by the history and magical design of the most beautiful playhouse in the country.

We are led by artists who see the world with distinctive clarity and whose ability to articulate what they see allows us to understand and engage with our world afresh. The company's programme includes original production, artist development and outreach; its work connecting on a local, national and international level.

In 2016, Bristol Old Vic marked its 250th birthday, celebrating with a season of work from the theatre's history as well as its future. Work also began on the final phase of the building's capital development, which will deliver a new foyer and studio theatre in 2018 designed by Stirling Prize winning architects Haworth Tompkins.

bristololdvic.org.uk

Act One

(MARC CHAGALL, an old man, sits on stage drawing in a little sketch book. His telephone rings and reluctantly he answers it.)

MARC: Hello?

FRANZ: Marc? It's me, Franz. I just wanted to go back to something we talked about this morning – would you agree that the iconography of your paintings resonates more as a complex chord, in which the immediately evident is instantaneously harmonised into a host of sublimated visions, as Breton put it in '41, that you give 'metaphor...plastic support in hypnagogic and eidetic imagery'?

Marc? ...Marc? What do you think?

MARC: Sorry... Was that a question?

FRANZ: Yes. Do you agree?

MARC: Yes...

FRANZ: Are you sure?

MARC: Yes. Hypna... Yes.

FRANZ: Alright. Now, an image – a recurring image – in your work is, of course, that of aerial lovers whose joy manifests itself in an almost palpable... frisson of colours and planes on the canvas. And yet, in their ecstasy, their attitude is somehow not exclusive. Their image becomes a kind of banner of spiritual potentiality under which everyone can march, even the sick at heart...

MARC: *(Interrupting.)* Franz, Franz... 'Banners'? 'Marching'...?

Franz, do you know why people paint?

FRANZ: Well... lots of reasons I suppose...

> *(MARC leaves the telephone hanging by its cord.)*

FRANZ: Marc...? Marc....?

> *(MARC rummages out a postcard and holds it up to the audience.)*

MARC: That's Vitebsk, my hometown, in 1914.

Two cathedrals, it had! And sixty synagogues...

> *(It's a black and white photograph of a town of many steeples over a river.)*

You know, they flattened it in the war, the Nazis – they pounded it to dust. And for those that never knew it, this is all that remains – black and white postcards...

FRANZ: *(Faintly.)* Marc, are you alright?

MARC: When some things are gone you thirst for their details in such a heart-breaking way... you feel an agony of need to remember... Perhaps the smell of a room in a house that has been razed to the ground for twenty years...

(He looks at the postcard.)

Shall I tell you a secret? In 1914, Vitebsk wasn't black and white at all!

(He shuts his eyes.)

The light was actually green in my eyes! And gold! And sometimes faintly lilac!

The air… smelt of dung! Because we all kept cows in our back yards! What else? I can smell… cinnamon in something baking… and smoke from the lamp – that wick needs a trim… and Mamma is frying fishballs…

(We hear fish frying, and other sounds. MARC recognises each like an old friend. We hear a watery rumble.)

My God, you know what that is don't you?! The samovar just starting to bubble!

(A clock ticks.)

That's our old clock, spending time like it had no end of it…

(A young woman begins to hum a song.)

That… that's Bella! Extraordinary! How like a girl she sounds! I suppose she almost was in 1914… You know, when she left school she was one of the four brightest students in all Russia! And for some reason, she took an interest in me…

(BELLA enters, singing playfully. She decides to confide in us.)

BELLA: Let me tell you about the first time I saw him. I'd gone to visit my friend, Thea, who's the daughter of our doctor. I waited two minutes on the doorstep before she answered the door to me. Then, for some reason, her face was red and shiny as a freshly washed radish! I barged in and plopped down onto a leather-bound sofa in her father's waiting room and began chattering on about some nonsense or other. But she was behaving very oddly… She shifted from foot to foot as if she needed to pay a visit and she seemed constantly on the verge of tittering in a high voice and floating up into the chandelier. And every few moments she stole a glance at the door of her father's surgery. So, Thea Brachman, who are you hiding away from me in there?

(A young MARC appears.)

My toes were as roots into the floor. Sheets of bluish flame rippled silently along the walls and ceiling and leapt into my hair.

His eyes. So blue. Splinters of heaven! They shot into me like arrows into a tree and made all my leaves quiver. Now I remembered Thea has already talked about him. He is a Jewish painter. He must encounter such misunderstanding here in sleepy Vitebsk. We must befriend him, she said. He needed models with open minds. Nude models…

(He steps forward. BELLA looks about to swoon.)

I was already running away, only I hadn't moved yet. 'Thea, I must go home…'

MARC: Why?

BELLA: he said,

MARC: You have such a beautiful smile, I want to draw you.

BELLA: Draw me? He was killing me! He'd climbed inside me and was running along beside me. My face was now all shiny radishes like Thea's. I looked down at the floor and saw my feet stepping onto the cobbles outside.

It seems as if we were courting the very next day. I remember sitting on a fallen tree by the river with him.

(MARC and she sit side by side. She shuts her eyes.)

We were too frightened to kiss, and yet I possessed with a passion the heat of half your body, from your left shoulder to your left ankle…

(Slowly, slowly, she turns to kiss him… but he gets up and goes.)

But then he went to Paris. To find greatness. Four years he's been gone and he writes hardly at all. Have you met greatness in the boulevards yet? Does she wear silk stockings…?

(Young MARC appears with a large brown leather suitcase in a railway carriage. He puts his head out of the window to speak to someone on the platform.)

MARC: Danke Herwarth. And Danke the others at 'Der Sturm' for me – and DANKE BERLIN! It was the best exhibition I've ever had! Now I can go back to Russia at last with my head held high!

(WALDEN leaves. MARC has another thought and calls him back.)

Oh… Walden! I'm only going to be in Russia for three months – I have my sister's wedding to go to next week, and my own the week after…! If she'll still have me… Auf wiedersehen!

(MARC calls him back again.)

Herwarth! I've wrapped one canvas and put it behind your desk. It's called 'Dedicated to my Fiancee'. On your life, don't sell that one – it's for her, my fiancé. Bella. Bella Rosenfeld. You can show it to people, just don't sell it. We'll pick it up on our way back to Paris. See you in three months!

(BELLA at home in Vitebsk.)

BELLA: Mother, why are you crying? Oh. Tishah b'Av again. I always forget. Must we actually weep every year? The Temple of Jerusalem fell so long ago – they'd be astonished to think we're still weeping now. Yes, I'm sure I'll understand one day, but it's summer outside, remember? It's time to pick blackberries… A new reason to weep? Mother you musn't find new reasons, you have enough old ones. Listen, if war can be declared so easily it must be a game. They'll call it off as quick again tomorrow.

(MARC hands her a letter.)

Marc...! from Berlin? *(She tears it open.)* He's coming home! He wants to marry me!

(MOTHER bursts into a new flood of tears.)

**

BELLA: Our wedding was within the month, at the house of my parents.

> *(BELLA is on display in her wedding dress. MARC slips in looking smart and uncomfortable, and is transfixed with embarrassment. They don't see each other yet.)*

MARC: Oh my God. Am I late? Look – the whole Sanhedrin is here. And I have as little to say as a corpse at his funeral, let alone the groom at his wedding, so I hope they don't expect any speeches...

BELLA: People come offering their doubts like gifts, smiling slyly,

'A painter, is he? Could he come and paint our dining room before Passover?' And I receive their doubts smiling equally slyly and stoke them onto a bonfire in my heart.

MARC: And look at all this! Stuffed trout, calf's foot jelly, fried udders... There's half an ark-full on these tables. Do you know they eat grapes in this house like my father eats onions...

> *(They see each other at last.)*

Bella. My dear Bella. It's a pity I'm no Veronese, what a sight you are!

Can you hear my eyes?

BELLA: Yes! Can you hear mine?

MARC: Yes. God help me, I feel like a clown!

BELLA: You look like one! You're beautiful. I want to waste the rest of my life with you!

MARC: Look at them... If only they knew. This isn't the crisp white start they think it is. My knowing you has already seeped backwards as well as forwards in time so my whole life is pervaded with the colour of loving you.

BELLA: Do you remember when I came to you that day...?

MARC: I lifted you in over the window sill.

BELLA: I could hear the neighbours clucking their tongues.

MARC: You'd brought a great bunch of flowers.

BELLA: I'd got up early and scrambled round the edge of town like a mad woman...

MARC: Your hair was all tangled with burrs!

BELLA: I'd picked 'til my hands were stinging...

MARC: You smelt of earth!

BELLA: ...blues and golds and pinks, then I wrapped them in all my shawls of colour...

MARC: And you'd robbed your own house of a cake and some of your mother's fried fish…

BELLA: Then I ran in the heat, along by the river.

MARC: I hadn't the faintest idea why you'd brought all this.

'Have you just come from the station or something?' I said.

BELLA: 'No. What day is it?'

MARC: 'You know how I lose track of the days Bella. Is it Tuesday? Wednesday…?'

BELLA: 'No, you fool! It's your BIRTHDAY!'

> *(She kisses him with a passion that shocks them both. MARC springs onto BELLA's shoulders and produces from his sleeve a bunch of flowers. MARC steps back to look at BELLA then reaches forward, as if to caress her face. Instead he tenderly tilts her head up and back to see her better. Inspired, he rushes to paint her.)*

You began to paint very fast… You… tugged me piece-by-piece under your brush… up off the ground, tugged back my head with your lips so that my eyes fell against the cupola of the church through the window and in my hands the flowers at the edge of my grip but they will never fall… you latched them there… and now they will always be on the edge of falling…

I was as far beyond doubt as the moon…

(Wedding music starts and they are forced to lead a dance. They are reluctant at first but are soon swept up in it. The dance gets frantic. At its height, MARC is apparently grabbed by BELLA's brothers and good-naturedly frog-marched towards the door.)

MARC: Where are we going? The party's only just started. What, in my own bed tonight? Are you mad, she's my wife. Stuff tradition. Wait…Bella… Bella…

**

(Two weeks later. We hear their laughter, singing, a metallic clanking, and MARC's voice all echoey. BELLA is feeding MARC milk from a tin pail. Autumn leaves fall now and then.)

BELLA: As Europe took itself to war, we took ourselves on honeymoon, to my family's dacha in the woods at Zaolshe.

MARC: No more. I'm going to explode.

BELLA: Drink it up. Every last drop. It's only three kopecs a bucket.

MARC: We'll remember this as our milkmoon.

BELLA: Milkmoon. Isn't that odd. Did I just say that to you?

MARC: No, I've just thought of it.

BELLA: I thought that yesterday, that this was our milkmoon. I've talked to you so much that I keep tripping over your thoughts in my head. We're like a pair of opera glasses. We choose to see the same things, to like the same things.

MARC: Like what? Tell me.

> *(As BELLA describes each thing, MARC brings it onto the stage.)*

BELLA: Big candles. Like the ones our mothers make to go in the shul on the Day of Atonement by weeping for the world and sealing their tears in wax on threads.

> *(MARC brings on a large lighted candle.)*

MARC: The strange Etrog from the citron tree whose fragrance wafts over your head in the sukkah at the Feast of Tabernacles and makes your mouth water.

> *(MARC brings on a large, lemon-like fruit.)*

BELLA: Wall-clocks with brass swords for pendulums that groan just before the hour then pound a chime that shocks you until you've forgotten again an hour later.

> *(MARC opens up his suitcase to reveal a large, old-fashioned clock.)*

MARC: Cows,

BELLA: cockerels,

MARC: fishes…

> *(There is a slight pause then MARC emerges with a large model of a cow under one arm, a fish under the other, and a large white cockerel on his head, perched on a hat. He sits on the floor next to BELLA and she strokes the cockerel while he strokes the cow.)*

When I painted these things in Paris, people looked at them like I'd dreamt them in a fever…

Oh Bella, I can't wait to show you Paris! I learnt everything I know about painting in my first ten minutes in the Louvre! And my friends will adore you! In fact, Cendrars will probably try to get you straight into bed with one of his outrageous poems…!

BELLA: When do we leave!?

(MARC looks worried. BELLA kisses him.)

MARC: I'll go straight back to Vitebsk and bribe the governor for our permits to travel at once.

(He shoots off.)

**

(BELLA finds large trunks ready to pack. A letter falls from above, like a leaf. She opens it and reads it. MARC comes back despondently.)

MARC: He laughed in my face and said Russia is sealed up like a tomb 'til the war ends.

It's chaos. The Jews on the border have been accused of spying for the Germans. They had to clear out in twenty-four hours or get shot. They're all trudging east now. Vitebsk is full to the brim.

I went to my mother's house for a cup of tea and there was an old man sat by the samovar…

(BELLA brings out the figure of him and sits him down.)

'Pardon me, sir, but who are you?' I said.

RABBI: You might have heard of me, my son. I am the Rabbi of Slousk.

MARC: The Rabbi of Slousk! With great holes in his boots and his coat all spattered with mud. The smell was unbelievable but he had the face of an angel. I said 'Rabbi',

RABBI: Yes my Son…

MARC: 'You just sit there and have a little rest. But you don't mind if I… If you… I mean, I'd like to…' I didn't know how to ask if I could paint him. I didn't want him to take offence and leave…

(The RABBI begins to snore.)

But I didn't have to ask in the end. He was sleeping like a child.

(He starts to paint the sleeping Rabbi of Slousk.)

Where will he go? He doesn't belong anywhere anymore.

(MARC takes the canvas and gently wraps the RABBI in it. BELLA helps and they hold him close like a sleeping child on their laps.)

BELLA: Oh… I'm afraid this has come for you too.

You've been called up.

(She hands him the letter.)

MARC: To fight for a country in which I'm a third-class citizen…!

BELLA: No. We'll go to Petersburg. I could get my brother to find you a position at the war office.

MARC: Jacov hates me.

BELLA: No he doesn't. Not too much. Oh Marc, you can't go to the front. You've got blue eyes and pink cheeks – you're the wrong colours to be a soldier. And you can carry on painting in Petersburg. We can pack all the things we love in Vitebsk into our minds and take them with us.

**

(MARC and BELLA arrive and set up their new home.)

BELLA: So we moved to a tiny flat up four flights of stairs, in starving Petersburg.

> *(He kisses her in a blaze of mauve light and leaves. The colour fades and a clock is heard ticking slowly.)*

BELLA: Here we lead a life where Marc goes off to work at half past seven and he doesn't come home until half past six. Eleven hours I sit and wait for him…

> *(A drip falls on BELLA's head from the ceiling.)*

The roof leaks in different places every day. I suppose it depends which way the wind is blowing…

> *(She moves several buckets to catch the drips.)*

I listen all day to the drips dripping… and the clock ticking… Our hearts are rusting in the damp eh, Mr Clock? Each tick is an uphill struggle for us.

(She oils the clock.)

This was a wedding present from my mother and father, you know. Did I tell you they have three jewellery shops in Vitebsk? But my mother spends her whole life behind the counter. My entire childhood I was sat alone upstairs with a book and a pastry and only the clock for company. Not much changed here then. Except now I have no pastries…

(Her stomach rumbles.)

But each night Marc comes home and we invent a new colour…

(MARC passes through and kisses her in a cloud of vermillion. Once he's gone, the colour fades.)

Then eleven hours more to myself.

It's all very well, I start to think. We may choose to see the same things, but he paints them and puts his name at the bottom of the canvas.

What should I do?

Everything seemed possible when I was studying in Moscow! I took acting classes with Stanislavsky you know! 'Love the art in yourselves,' he said. Under his eyes the feelings would stream out of us like sticky cobwebs and bind us all together…!

But here I have to love the art inside myself alone. Then another night comes…

(MARC passes through and kisses her in lime.)

But this morning…

(She listens to herself.)

I could just… hear a new tick ticking…

(We catch it too now.)

…tiny but twice as fast, already starting to fill all the gaps inside me.

So I thought, I had better do something for myself before the day ends. So I've dug out this old notebook and I've started writing, painting in Yiddish, the most colourful you can be in black and white – not much, but something in my own hand at least, before it's too late.

(We see MARC walking.)

MARC: I've always hated Petersburg… Even daylight is in short supply here. It's so cold. I must smile at passers-by just to feel the warmth of their smiles in return.

(He smiles at someone.)

They must think I'm a lunatic.

(He sits at a desk.)

And every morning I have to feel grateful to Jacov for saving me from the Front. All day long the clock gnaws me like a bone.

(BELLA appears before him in a haze of cyan.)

Bella suffers it all without a word…

But then she did study philosophy at university, I suppose.

And history. And literature. Her thesis was on Dostoyevsky…

(She chops up a chair and feeds it into a stove.)

I'm painting, in secret at Goldberg's place, a series of kisses for her. Does she actually know? Everything I've ever made is for her…

(She fades away.)

Now Jacov comes. 'Tell me please, what does the number of conscripts from Dvinsk now stand at? Well?'

'I don't know.'

(JACOV sweeps everything off the desk.)

'Imbecile! Can't you even <u>try</u> to deserve your position?'

What joy it is to escape at midday!

(He leaves his desk.)

But something is happening out here... you can start to feel the motions of time through the soles of your feet...

(Seismic clockwork accelerates.)

The snow is melting and so are the food queues, they're flowing down the Nevsky Prospect with banners for peace and bread and freedom...

(Gunfire. Panic. The clockwork whirrs faster. MARC is swept to and fro and must shout over the crowd.)

The Imperial Guard are firing into the crowd...

My... my hat...! And now, apparently, the Volunsky Regiment has revolted! All sixteen thousand!

What...? They say... the Tsar has abdicated!

Hooray...! What are we cheering for now? A Provisional Government! Hooray! Excuse me... I must get back to work... Hooray...!

(MARC pushes through. The noise is fainter inside the Ministry.)

But back inside, every soul had left his desk. Even Jacov has gone, the turncoat!

Freedom! My God... Today, for the first time since
Catherine the Great, a poor Jew is free in Petersburg!
No more permits for me now!

(He run back out into the din.)

HOOOORRRAAAYYY!

(A bullet narrowly misses his head.)

There's a different mood out on Liteynay now...
Soldiers are running everywhere with the badges
ripped off their coats – wild horses won't drag
them back to the Front... They've broken open the
prisons...

(Glass smashes.)

And the shop windows. They're helping themselves
to silver forks... And why are they hauling a coat up
that lamp post? My God... a policeman... strung up
by the neck...

I must get off the street... Goldberg's is just around
the corner...

*(He ducks into a side street to bump straight into a gang
of men.)*

Good evening friends...

VOICE: Jew or not?

MARC: Excuse me...?

VOICE: JEW OR NOT?

MARC: Me? A Jew! You... you insult me kamerad!

VOICE: Alright. Get along.

> *(MARC turns. A shot rings out behind him and he falls in terror. They laugh. MARC scuttles away.)*

**

(BELLA waits, seated, for MARC. He enters sheepishly and sits too, apart from her.)

MARC: You look a bit slimmer.

BELLA: Now, on the fourth day, you come and see your daughter for the first time. There's no possible reason I could understand, but I want to hear you try to explain...

MARC: An exhibition. Nadezhda Dobchina is going to give me an exhibition...!

Bella, Nadezhda Dobchina...!

BELLA: I don't give a damn about Nadezhda Dobchina!

MARC: This could be my chance in my own country at last! I've been painting day and night since I heard...

BELLA: Painting!!

MARC: I thought you'd understand...

BELLA: It hurt *so* <u>much</u>...

MARC: Never, for one moment, did I mean to hurt you...

BELLA: Not my feelings you imbecile! Here...!

(She points at herself. MARC is abashed.)

I can still hardly walk! And you come twittering to me about Nadezhda Dobchina!

MARC: I'm sorry my work seems so trivial to you by comparison...

BELLA: Marc!

MARC: But honestly, do you think what I do happens painlessly? If I stopped pushing I'd never paint another picture again. And what would I mean without my paintings Bella? Nothing, because my father doesn't own three jewellery shops he carries barrels of herring all day...

BELLA: I've told you a thousand times, that doesn't matter to me...

MARC: You'd never have looked at me twice without my paintings!

BELLA: People, Marc... you, your daughter! That's what's matters most to me. Not paintings...!

(A bottle crashes through the window with some paper stuffed in the neck. At first MARC and BELLA panic, thinking it's a MOLOTOV cocktail. The baby begins to cry. BELLA picks her up and tries to soothe her.)

MARC: A message...

'Marc Chagall is invited to become Director of Fine
Art in the new Commissariat of Culture.'
My God… Look! Mayakowsky for poetry,
Meyerhold for theatre, Marc Chagall for Fine Art!!!

BELLA: You can't do it…

MARC: Why not?

BELLA: You'd stop painting.

MARC: A moment ago you didn't care about my painting!

My God, Mother Russia is asking a peasant Jew to be
a minister… And of painting!

BELLA: We must go back to Vitebsk…

MARC: Vitebsk? No. The Revolution wants me. Me, who
paints green cows and… flying rabbis! The New
Russia wants to speak to her people with painted
speeches!

BELLA: Your paintings aren't speeches Marc! Let's go
back. Please? Maybe in Vitebsk they'll let you start
a little art school or something. You have to keep
painting. And I need to go home.

MARC: Go home? Perhaps. Yes!! An arts school in
Vitebsk for people like me! I could teach the droshky
drivers to paint portraits of their horses!

BELLA: *(To the baby.)* It's alright my darling… everything
is alright…

> *(MARC finally seems to notice the child and strokes her head.)*

Maybe if she'd been a boy you'd have found time to come.

MARC: Have you named her without me?

BELLA: Only what we talked about.

MARC: Ida?

BELLA: For your mother.

MARC: Ida...

> (BELLA has tried to start packing, holding IDA.)

MARC: Bella... let me hold her.

> (BELLA hands over the baby and continues to pack. MARC dandles IDA for a while and then makes her a pair of paper wings. He flies her over to BELLA who wraps her tightly in a blanket.)

She's not a vase – maybe we should uncover her mouth a little.

> (BELLA uncovers IDA's mouth and watches MARC carry IDA off. She gathers their luggage then finds her notebook. MARC has torn the paper wings from the pages of her writing.)

**

(It is the week before the first anniversary of the October Revolution. They are back in Vitebsk. BELLA holds IDA in her arms. MARC is stood on a chair to practise a speech.)

MARC: You are the sign-painters and house-painters of Vitebsk.

BELLA: They'll already know who they are Marc.

MARC: I have called you all together to ask you to join my school. Shut down your sign studios, shut down your daub-shops. All the orders can be sent to the school. We will split the work up between us, fathers and sons working shoulder to shoulder. Now, next week is the first anniversary of the October Revolution. We intend to commemorate it in a big way. We plan to erect 350 red banners, 7 triumphal arches, and to repaint the shops and trolleys in the main square in red…and purple, and yellow, and green…

Listen… Let me say it plainly.

There's never been a moment like this before. People like us… history has always sat on our heads like the lid of a tomb. But look! That stone has broken! And men like us have risen through the cracks overnight, pushed up by talent and vision alone!

So let's use this moment, my friends, let's make our dear Vitebsk look more splendid that anyone's ever dared imagine! Above all, let us be proud – because our gifts belong to Russia and, at last, Russia belongs to us…!

**

(MARC and BELLA are at the parade on the anniversary of the October Revolution. There are banners with a blue horse, green cows, goats, etc. There is fervent singing of a revolutionary song. MARC believes in it all and is ecstatic. BELLA believes in MARC and is less ecstatic.)

INTERVAL

Act Two

(MARC crosses the stage on the way to his school. He looks worried and is lost in thought. He fails to notice a newly-erected concrete bust of KARL MARX as he passes it, but comes back to look at it moments later, in disgust.)

MARC: Look at it. There used to be a bench here where I kissed my wife. Passionately. After dark. Now this. Do you know it's so ugly it frightens passing horses and children in prams... Now, listen.

(He reads from a local newspaper.)

'Let's not make fools of ourselves... People of Vitebsk, did you know that 45,000 pairs of underpants could have been made from the banners at Saturday's march?' I suppose the learned Bolshevik would have advised the burghers of Florence to squeeze their fat arses into underpants tailored from Raphael's Madonnas. Listen, 'Comrade Chagall's multicoloured airborne farmyard made a mystical bachannal out of the whole proceedings.' The cow is green because I like it that way – he still cheers for the proletariat. There is no mystery, or do they need me to dig up Mr Marx to come and explain it to them? That isn't the half of it. I thought my school needed revolutionary painters. 'Men from the capital for the province.' So I invited Malevich the Suprematist, Lissitzky, Alexander Romm – to teach in my school. Me. I was responsible for flinging all these crabs in the same basket. Then this morning, when I went there, a banner had been draped across the front of my school saying, SUPREMATIST ACADEMY. Malevich has started a mutiny! They've voted to expel me within twenty-four hours. All this time I've laid down my own paint-brush to build this school, to be expelled from it like a naughty schoolboy. I don't want to deny what they see. Why must they deny my eyes? Must we all paint the same way? Has the Revolution only freed us to fight like dogs until there's only one pack left, composed of the ugliest with the longest teeth?

Right. Let them fight. I know what I'm going to do...

(He starts to leave. BELLA comes in out of breath.)

BELLA: Marc...

MARC: Malevich has taken over my school.

BELLA: Marc

MARC: Never mind. You will be pleased to hear, I'm going to spend the afternoon painting...!

BELLA: Marc – the Cheka have come to my parents' shop. They're... they're taking everything ... even the silver from the dining room table. They're levering the safes out of the walls and smashing the clocks...

MARC: Why now?

BELLA: I don't know, there's been an attempt on Lenin's life or something... but it's just an excuse – they're after the money. Thieves come in uniform nowadays.

MARC: I'm sorry.

(He starts to leave again.)

BELLA: Where are you going?

MARC: I told you – back to work.

BELLA: But... I need you to help me!

MARC: How? I'm a painter.

BELLA: Your name, your position... they must count for something...

MARC: They've expelled me from the school!

BELLA: So, what...? You're going off to paint flowers or something?

MARC: If I feel like it.

BELLA: You... child!! Can't you see? They're losing everything they've worked for in their whole lives!

MARC: What matters most to me now is to capture something precious and fleeting for eternity. Not silverware.

BELLA: What matters now is to do the right thing by those you love!

MARC: Would Veronese have painted 'The Marriage at Cana' if he was worrying about cutlery…?

BELLA: Shut up about Veronese for once! Please! We need you now. You can paint tomorrow…

MARC: You see, that is just your mistake. For you there is <u>always</u> something else more important and that is why you will <u>never</u> be a writer!

(BELLA runs away.)

MARC: Bella! Bella!

(He follows her.)

**

MARC: We couldn't stay in Vitebsk.

Not long after we left, my father was crushed by the wheels of a truck while still loading barrels of herring after all these years, but we didn't go back for the funeral. We never went back and the world we knew disappeared forever.

We went to Moscow to live every day on nothing but black bread and kasha made with millet.

Then a friend found me a job at last, painting scenery at the New Jewish Theatre. Bella was intoxicated.

(BELLA can be heard down a corridor, getting a light-hearted lesson from a young man on how to recite a Yiddish poem.)

BELLA speaks in Yiddish.

Keyner veyst es nisht, afile du aleyn –

Az vu ikh zol nisht geyn, trog ikh mit zikh dayn blik,

Vi a kameye mit an ayngekritstn shprukh,

Dem shprukh tsum goyrl azoy noent un azoy vayt fun glik.

<u>*MARC sings*</u>

No one knows it, not even you
That wherever I go, I carry your glance, Like an amulet
with an engraved spell,
The spell for a fate so near and so far.

> *(Now BELLA opens a door into the dark room where MARC*
> *is brooding in a pool of light from a work lamp.)*

BELLA: Where's our cave-man?

MARC: I'm glad someone's cheerful… Where's Ida?

BELLA: With Mikhoels. He was giving us lessons in
Yiddish acting! But now I think he's teaching Ida a
very rude song…!

MARC: How risqué…

Well… these actor types are so tiringly colourful,
aren't they?

BELLA: Are we perhaps a little jealous!?

MARC: Come off it! But don't you hate the theatre sometimes? With its endless dreary words… and all that pointless moving about…

BELLA: How else are they supposed to tell the story?!

MARC: I don't know, I just wish they'd stand still sometimes and let the audience look at the scenery.

BELLA: Well I think they're wonderful… I wish I could join them!

MARC: But who would look after Ida?

BELLA: Anyway. I'm too old. Solomon says they do two hours physical training every morning.

MARC: I know. Upstairs. It feels like they're trooping about on my skull. It's impossible to paint…

BELLA: How is it going?

> (MARC shines the light at the bare wall.)

> <u>MARC sings</u>

> *No one knows it, not even you*
> *But since the day when I came to this town*
> *Longing has been roaming over all the streets*
> *And all the trees are greener with a new secret.*

MARC: Not a doodle.

BELLA: Marc… What's done is done. Lay down this great… sack of old troubles you carry round all the time. In fact, where is it…?

(She pretends to search him for it and tickles him at the same time.)

Let me take it away now!

MARC: Don't... Bella... STOP! I don't care anymore.

(She stops and sits by him.)

My sister has written. She says they're closing all the synagogues in Vitebsk – They've turned the one where my father used to pray into a shoe factory! She says it's a blessing he died when he did because the sight would have killed him... I can't stop feeling how easily his poor life was snuffed out. Fifty-seven years and the truck driver didn't even notice and drove away whistling. And now we can't even afford a stone for him. When less than two years ago they were hanging my paintings in the Winter Palace! But now it seems my work ... it actually embarrasses people! What did they call it...? 'Powdered rococo'!

BELLA: Don't take any notice of that...

MARC: Nobody wants us here anymore Bella...

So how can I paint?

BELLA: But Marc we've found ourselves in the one place where we <u>are</u> wanted! My God Marc! The actors... It's astonishing! They're... they're swallowing our whole world and locking it in their bones! When Mikhoels moves on stage you can see it all there in front of you!

> *BELLA sings in Yiddish.*

Keyner veyst es nisht, afile du aleyn –
Nokh zayt dem tog, vos kh'bin in ot der shtot,
Geyt di benkshaft um do iber ale gasn
Un ale beymer zenen griner mit a nayem sod

BELLA: Come on. Take part.

> What better memorial could you make for your
> father?!

> *BELLA sings in Yiddish.*

Keyner veyst es nisht, afile du aleyn –
Az, ven es eynzamen mit mir di shoen shitile,
Dan fir ikh mit di fingershpitsn iber mayne lipn
Un nem fun zey arop dayn nomen, vi a tfile.

> *MARC sings.*

No one knows it, not even you
That when I am alone in my quiet hours,
Then do I lead my fingertips over my lips
And take from them your name, like a prayer.

> *(MARC shakes his head and stares into the dark.*

> *BELLA is seized with purpose. She casts the working light*
> *against the wall once more and stands in it, throwing a giant*
> *shadow of herself there. With sudden waves of her arms she*
> *sweeps MARC onto his feet, then flicks up his arms so he*
> *throws first his palette then his brush into the air and must*
> *struggle to catch them.*

She begins to recite the Yiddish poem and the rhythms, the taste of the words, are irresistible. She sways and sweeps, driving MARC's arms into the air repeatedly with bolts of her electricity.

Then, suddenly, MARC is provoked and swipes back, knocking one of her arms into the air. He begins to recite the poem too, painting her body into a dance. He moves closer and closer until he steps before the light and his shadow lies over hers. He kisses her. She steps away and he continues to paint.

Satisfied, she watches him. So absorbed in painting now, he is unaware when a hatch opens and admits a slice of light bearing a letter. BELLA reads it, a frown growing on her face. She puts the letter in MARC's hand. He continues to work a moment, to finish something, then looks at it.)

MARC: It's from Rubiner in Berlin… It seems I'm famous in Germany! My paintings have launched a movement there called… 'Expressionism'!

(He reads.) 'Walden's sold all of your paintings at very good prices but don't expect to see any of the money – he thinks you're probably dead in the war or the revolution, so the glory alone will make a fine memorial.' I don't believe it – That means he's sold your wedding present… Bella…?

(He notices now that BELLA has slipped away. He looks back at his painting.)

MARC: From that time forward my fame abroad grew and grew, but I was never embraced in my motherland as I yearned to be. But I still think those paintings in the Jewish Theatre were the best I ever did.

We left Russia soon after and, like millions of others, we didn't stop wandering for the next twenty years. And with each step further from home, the older we grew.

(BELLA returns looking aged. She sits, puts on glasses and gets out her notebook and pen.)

When news reached us, how the Nazis were destroying every last atom of Jewish life in the Pale, Bella started writing in Yiddish again, about home.

(We hear what BELLA is writing. MARC makes coffee in the background and watches her.)

BELLA: *(She speaks the first line in Yiddish, then repeats it in English.)*

'The station had always worried me. The waiting room was always full of agitation. It was so crowded I was afraid the whole population of Vitebsk was leaving, bag and baggage. What would it be like, a city without people? Perhaps the houses too had been packed up and sent off somewhere.

Suddenly the station master appeared in the doorway.

"First call!" he shouted and swung the bell.

I didn't know which faces to concentrate on. Suddenly all of these people seemed near and dear to me. And they were going away and leaving me alone. Would they ever come back? What would happen to the town?

The engine roared and swallowed up carriage after carriage of passengers. The train was taking leave of our city in a cloud of smoke. Sparks flew, flames spurted. The engine wheezed and started to pull the carriages one after another along behind it. The stoker's naked back gleamed as if he was in hell.

The train was on its way, and I was going back to the town as to a deserted house. Would the trees still be there? Everything is silent, I thought. Is Vitebsk still there…?'

MARC: Here.

> (He puts down her coffee gently, but still startles her. She shuts her notebook and smiles at him.)

BELLA: Thank you.

> (She labels the book and puts it away carefully.)

MARC: You're more like a squirrel every day. Why so tidy all of a sudden?

BELLA: So you'll know where everything is.

> (BELLA puts on a record, 'I'm Making Believe' by the Ink Spots, and she and MARC dance slowly in each other's arms.)

MARC: We were staying at a place outside New York called Cranberry Lake. The birch trees there always reminded us of Zaolshe, where we spent our Milkmoon. One day, after swimming in the lake, Bella fell ill.

**

(MARC paces, BELLA sits huddled.)

MARC: We should have stayed at the hospital…

BELLA: But the nuns…

MARC: They're just women in funny clothes.

BELLA: Their hats scared me…

MARC: They were kind.

BELLA: So why did they ask me, 'what religion'?

MARC: They were just filling in a form…

BELLA: You know I saw that sign at the hospital in Beaver Lake…

MARC: That was Beaver Lake…

BELLA: 'Only white Christians welcome.'

MARC: But Bella, we have to go back…

BELLA: It's just a sore throat…

MARC: If only I could make myself understood. I should have learnt English.

BELLA: Is Ida coming?

MARC: As fast as she can…

BELLA: You liar!

MARC: What?

BELLA: You told me I was the first nude you had ever seen. I only had the courage to take off my dress because Thea Brachman had done it for you the week before.

MARC: So, it means I know exactly how much more beautiful you are than Thea Brachman…

BELLA: Is Ida coming?

MARC: Yes.

BELLA: Talk to me.

MARC: I am.

BELLA: Say something nice.

MARC: I can't think of anything nice…

BELLA: Sit with me then. You're making me dizzy.

(He sits by her and feels her forehead.)

MARC: Bella you're burning! *(He mops her face.)* We *must* go back!

BELLA: But the nuns…

MARC: Damn the nuns…! I'm so scared…

BELLA: Hush… Something nice…

MARC: 'Nice'…!

BELLA: Something happy… Please.

MARC: Alright… think, think… the happiest must be surely that day when you came to my room. You know, when you surprised me…

BELLA: Yes! I did it so well!

MARC: You did. I had no idea.

BELLA: Tell me.

MARC: Surely you're sick of it…

BELLA: Of hearing about my brilliance? Never.

MARC: Well. It was a very hot day. I had the window open and the shutters half closed and you tapped on them and I lifted you in.

You always brought different flowers. This time they were all wild and delicate and smelling of earth…

BELLA: My notebooks…

MARC: Yes. And you were all bedecked in your party clothes. You were panting and carrying several brightly wrapped parcels. 'Have you come from the station?' I said to you.

'No,' you said, 'What day is it today?'

'I don't know. Is it Tuesday or Wednesday?' – I never knew what day it was.

'It's your birthday!' you said!

That moment on that day... I needed no more perfect moment than that...

> *(BELLA gets up and walks away. MARC becomes old before our eyes. He takes up the telephone receiver once more and speaks into it.)*

MARC: It was just a streptococcus throat infection. But it was the war, you see – the doctor had no penicillin to give her. She went into a coma and she died before Ida could even get there...

You know, afterwards, when I read her notebooks, I found them so...vivid! And I was startled somehow that her view was so close and yet so different to my own. But what a fool! Had it never occurred to me that though we saw the same things, she saw them with her own eyes? And my heart broke again because she had died so hidden – like all those other Yiddish souls, snuffed out before half their light was shed...

Of course, Ida translated her work so beautifully into French and I made those drawings to go with it and now it's published, thank God. So, we uncovered her a little to the world...

But to touch her life with my drawings…! You know, when I drew my arm around her head, I could actually feel the weight of her hair on my wrist… and the warmth from the back of her head…

What greater purpose could my work have than that?

Forgive me Franz… What was your question?

FRANZ: Never mind. We can pick up again tomorrow. Ida sends a kiss by the way.

MARC: Send her one from me then. A nice one!

FRANZ: Goodnight Marc.

MARC: Goodnight Franz.

> *(MARC sits alone and quiet. He fetches out a tub and munches from the contents.)*

Fishballs. Vava is a better cook than a model – and these are delicious.

She'll never pose for me. She gets 'ants in her pants!' Is that what you say?!

I suppose 'being a good model' isn't a wedding vow. Perhaps it should be for the wives of painters…

> *(But now a voice is heard singing playfully and BELLA comes, wearing a purple dress and wings all covered in her own writing. She sits with MARC companionably.)*

BELLA: Your breath smells of fishballs.

MARC: Have one. Then you won't notice.

(She eats one.)

BELLA: Not as good as mine…

MARC: I'm sorry.

BELLA: Don't be. They're only fishballs.

MARC: I'm not sorry about the fishballs…

End.